MINGUS TAKES (3)

3 One Acts

Aishah Rahman

BROADWAY PLAY PUBLISHING INC
New York
www.broadwayplaypublishing.com
info@broadwayplaypublishing.com

First printing: May 2012
I S B N: 978-0-88145-515-1

Book design: Marie Donovan
Page make-up: Adobe Indesign
Typeface: Palatino
Printed and bound in the U S A

ALSO BY AISHAH RAHMAN

Plays

LADY DAY: A MUSICAL TRAGEDY
THE MOJO AND THE SAYSO
ONLY IN AMERICA
TALE OF MADAME ZORA
UNFINISHED WOMEN CRY IN NO MAN'S LAND
WHILE A BIRD DIES IN A GILDED CAGE

One Acts

IF ONLY WE KNEW
THE LADY AND THE TRAMP
SPEAKER'S HEAD

Novel

Pigmentocracy Blues

Memoir

Chewed Water

Libretto

ANYBODY SEEN MARIE LAVEAU?

INTRODUCTION

Charles Mingus, Jr was born April 22, 1922 and died January 5, 1979. He was a virtuoso jazz composer and bassist who protested racial injustice through his music that ranged from traditional jazz and blues to Be-Bop and Free Jazz.

MINGUS TAKES (3) is dedicated to Mingus's ingeniousness, his humor and revolutionary spirit and his great contribution to American Classical Music more commonly labeled Jazz.

SPEAKER'S HEAD

A monologue

SPEAKER'S HEAD was first produced by Perishable Theatre (Mark Lerman, Artistic Director) in Providence, Rhode Island running from 10 April-17 May 2003. The actor and creative contributors were:

SPEAKER .... Bob Jaffe

Director .... Don Mays

Design .... Monica Shinn

CHARACTERS

SPEAKER, *a man*

A bass player, hidden in the shadows is SPEAKER's *alter ego who, improvising on his bass, carries on a musical interchange with* SPEAKER, *emphasizing, agreeing, cajoling, laughing, throughout* SPEAKER's *monologue whenever the spirit moves him.*

(The theater is in total blackness except for intermittent flashes of blinding light throughout in which audience is able to catch revealing glimpses of SPEAKER*.)*

(Audible deep signs of deep exasperation, multiple grunts, throat clearing with subtle changes in intonation get louder and more frantic. When he finally talks, SPEAKER*'s sentences are not fluid but in spurts followed by meaningful pauses etc. Finally, he blurts out, unable to control.. himself…)*

SPEAKER: I'm…agonizing…to…speak…talk to… YOU…but I'm not supposed to…not yet…supposed to wait for the control freaks running around to give me a signal…before I… And they won't even let me know what it is…is…it…is…what… "You'll know…you can't miss it" …. "just wait"….not until I get a signal…can…I…address…YOU…my right… dutyandobligation…to address YOU…and I have to… to…waitfor…a…damn…poppycock signal…sometimes all the do's and don't's just…get my gauge up to… It's just that I'm pining to…Just me…and you…no media misinterpreting…slanting… You know…like you…I have my moments too when I feel misunderstood.

But when I feel like that…I just….stick to my guns and turn to my Cat. She knows…she knows…keeps me from feeling buffallowed…knows…how I feel…just nuzzling up to her cold nose…looking into her steady eyes makes everything alright all of you Americans out there who own Cats know what I mean.

Back in yesteryear…when I possessed…a smaller and
lesser abusive weapon it was very dear to me to hunt
at the break of dawn…rounds fired at daybreak rouse
the spirit but…when the varmint hunting-at-night-bug
bit me a couple years back it was mind shattering…
that's when I became a wildcatter…that's…when I…
when…I…attained true enlightenment…content at last
in my own element.

Cat actually helps me to see…varmints better…in the
dark. No fits and starts…I made her eyes extra bright
she goes…striaght to the heart…from her very first
shot…in the dark.

*(A picture of a large amber cat eye is projected in the total
darkness.)*

SPEAKER: I designed her strictly to help me see better
in low light. I made her cat's eye extra bright by giving
it supersight with an oversized lens and then tinting it
with just a splash of amber. Then I made her exit pupil
large…and increased her eye relief…in the dark.

*(The cat eye begins to roam randomly, stopping as if sighting
an individual audience member.)*

When all is said and done…I like to shoot in low light
situations…very…low…light…situations.

(A long, uncomfortable pause)

SPEAKER: Most varmints have a doom reaction when
they find themselves in a dark location and Boom and
boom and boom again quick as Jack Robinson, they are
hit where they ain't a patron saint!

Cat and I have a romance…the sighting, the waiting,
the savoring, her one and only kiss of death shot for
the heart of varmint I select. On my oath I protect…
revere…and respect…Cat.

My first bout with wildcat fever was with the .22-250 I had one built up real regal only to lose my status as a wildcatter cause it became legal.

I don't know about you...I'm willing to bet dollars to case quarters you're just like me and you see...I am your...type of American that, like you I'm willing to bet, does a difficult thing just because...I...can. So What?

I like to prove...my mettle and always choose to settle on the highest mountain top...just to prove I am in fine fettle.

You...might as well admit it...yes... You, don't' look away...I mean YOU and the person beside you...and the one in front...and the guy...or gal...in back of you whose hand you brush...and feet you can't help but step on...whose behind brushes you on the way to a scat, whose breathing...right now this very minute is in time with yours right now...as... You...breathe... in...and...out...inhaling...exhaling...every student, teacher, cowboy, soldier, lawman and housewife, every true American, the one thing we all yearn for is a custom rife built from our own specifications. Praise the Lord and pass the ammunitions!

Lately, I been hurting all over to upgrade and modernize my varmint arsenal. I want the whole enchilada. Yada, yada, yada.

I like a walking gun and would easily build my own... but trouble is...blasted gunmakers are bursting my bubble...with all the new rifle cartridges we've seen... introduced on the markets...these past few years... it brings me to salty tears...I say if gunmakers...keep on making everything legal...I say...I might as well be hunting eagles.

I am lusting to upgrade my M-16 to a Bushmaster XM15 A3 M4 so and make the semiautomatic as

automatic as a military rifle which I figger allows
multiple rounds to be fired with a pull of the trigger.
Let those who would attack the Second Amendment
snigger, an armed American citizen is a safe American
citizen After all peace is more likely if you know the
next fellow…or gal…is as armed to the teeth and feet
and as good a marksman as you…this…insures… A
state of good will and peace among you and me.

Me and you…let's understand something…about you
and me about each other. We must understand that
you and me…uh…WE that's it…yes we…are tarred
with the same brush. In God *We* Trust…you and me…
we…sleep the sleep of the just. No four flusher cloud
dusters, coming on like gang busters can weaken
America's cover or divide and conquer the lawks the
doves amoungst us , trust us, one for oil, oil for one,
thick and thicker, not one of us differs, we keep stiff
lips stiffer, we keep the peace and avoid early decease,
no leaps for you and me in order not to weep.

To be blunt, America is bearing the brunt and all is
unquiet on our Western Front.

A reign of terror? The more the merrier, trial and
error, a money-grabber, next door neighbor, be a back
stabber, call a number, jibber-jabber, name rank and
serial number, slave labor, don't look for the union
label.

Opportunity is a dead soldier, a knight in shinning
armor, a horse of a different color, blue collar you can
bet your bottom dollar, keeping his head above water,
led like a lamb to slaughter, at the end of his tether,
birds of a feather…flock…together.

As I was saying, Captains of Industry, In this Hour
of the Cash Box thick skinned thin skinned get their
second wind, go like the wind, into the teeth of the
wind, spitting into the wind throw caution to the wind,

crash landing the left hand doesn't know what the right hand steals...sorry feels...what the right hand feels, have a fling live like a king,

A crash landing, double dealing, keep the ball rolling, make a killing, the sky is falling, it's all in the calling, collective bargaining day of reckoning.

In the Land of Lincoln, swallow hook, line and sinker, Florida hot sun melts butterfingers, slippery election gives voters the fingers, Supreme court selection has sticky fingers Cross my fingers, no hard feelings, count your fingers...uh...blessings.

Bad moon rising, Black clouds on the horizon, bombs of contention, an ounce of prevention, military invention, necessity is a mother.

Let me make it perfectly clear, America is hell-bent, full of incident, and lacking a gentleman's agreement, lacking the red-carpet treatment, even if we get the silent treatment, moment to moment, on the spur of the moment and for our halfway indecent allies, not one red cent, we will fold up our tent and prepare for our unilateral event.

America will not back out, faced with a lockout, we won't shutout, bow out, but rather we will dish it out. My good ole intuition tells me War will be good for expanding America nutrition... History agrees with me... Who ever heard of Sushi...before Nagasaki? In '45 Truman's...instruction...made it clear then... And now I say it again....our glorious weapons of mass destruction...keeps us victorious...a perfect selection... for the world's protection...the only way we can peace out.

Therefore at an ungodly hour, at the eleventh hour, in the midnight hour, the happy hour, a balance of power under one's own power. Do I have to spell it out?

We absolutely must be able to…absolutely…destroy…
early during this…pre-crisis…period…to completely
and definitely foil…to controil, uh control those who
wickedly plan America's destruction who wickedly
plan…behind our backs…as we plan to attack…I call
upon you to stop their evil peace scheming…to pursue,
and subdue, to not ruminate, but annihilate in order to
expurgate our righteous fears, as we must.

Some (not all) varmints insist on no capitulation from
their ancestors uncivilized and wicked concepts of
sovereign terrain and they refrain…from accepting our
democratic concept of eminent world domain.

(Slowly the lights begin to go up.)

SPEAKER: And now, I think, I see some kind of strange
movement… Let me leave you with these final words.

There must not be any Trojan horses hiding in plain
sight in America.

We must attack and controil…uh control, control…
varmints who do not like us at hone and abroad.

Our left hand must know what weapons our right
hand is carrying.

And in our democracy a CAT may look at a king.

My fellow Americans…rest insured…that…you
have…my very warm…assurances…of my continued
high assurances…uh…considerations…and and
ministrations and…and…and and and—

VOICE: YOU'RE ON!

SPEAKER: —and..and God better Bless America!

(SPEAKER raises his rifle triumphantly over his head.)

(Curtain)

END OF PLAY

IF ONLY WE KNEW

An on going urban drama
with jazz and movement in
one act

IF ONLY WE KNEW was first produced by
Perishable Theater (Mark Lerman, Artistic Director)
in Providence, Rhode Island running from 12 April-17
May 2003. The cast and creative contributors were:

ABOULAYE .... Jonathan Mahon
NARRATOR .... Kevin Gibbs
MUSICIAN .... Randy Ashe

Director .... Don Mays
Design .... Monica Shinn

CHARACTERS & SETTING

ABOULAYE, *a Guinean street peddler*
NARRATOR, *his African-American* alter ego
BLIND STREET CORNER BASS PLAYER

Place: New York City, 21st Century

PLAYWRIGHTS NOTES

It should be difficult, at times, to differentiate between Aboulaye and Narrator; the two characters should appear with the help of music and movement to melt into one another, and actors should be lithe, able to move well.

(The stage is bare. The BASSIST *plays quiet, spiritual music that evokes the dawn for a long time.)*

NARRATOR: *(Over the music)* Morning prayer, 5:30 A M.

ABOULAYE: America! I love it! I love it! I just love it! love New York, love the Bronx and I love sneakers. I love America where everyday's tomorrow.

NARRATOR: Mid day prayer, twelve noon.

Your behind hits the door, when you bend over, you fill the tiny vestibule as you lace your right sneaker that is always coming untied. Today you are wearing your Air Jordan that light up green in the dark. Bon. Cool. As you straighten up your elbows brush against the mailboxes on your right and you quickly open the door and go down the one, two, three, four

(Music stops.)

NARRATOR: short steps, stopping to look up at the woman who sits above you, looking, looking. Always looking day and night, looking out her window.

ABOULAYE: Gonna, gonna take the 6 train Hurry hurry hurry gotta jet downtown. Number 6 to one four street can't be late don't be late it won't wait go to sell got to yell money money money got to get some run don't be late african boy black boy Frenchie cool boy glowing feet shinning, five feet six inches of thin jaguar skin nine eyes neon footed quick change artist catch the hurry hurry no 6, stop gotta dash, gotta book gotta split from the Bronx bush to downtown from north to south from east to west to downtown where the action is, money flows everything goes, through Harlem, through midtown downtown, is your town money money flows everyone knows...can't be late money wont wait.

(Rushing music for several beats that stops suddenly.)

NARRATOR: You make a bee line through your black and tan neighborhood where February turns brown to ash where everyone moves aside for your morning dash to the high in the sky train tracks rising above the rows of two story red brick doll houses on either side with four steps leading up to a tiny vestibule where two full grown adults cannot stand in at the same time.

ABOULAYE: Hurry!

NARRATOR: Hurry! Hurry! Hurry on downtown to the east side take the 6 to 14th cross over and go east young man don't be late, cause money won't wait

(BASSIST: A Long interval of rising "subway music" that finally diminishes underneath the following:)

ABOULAYE: Hurry hurry hurry hurry do I have my wallet? Hope I didn't forget my wallet wallet got to have my wallet need my wallet, there she is, good old Baji right here in my hand

NARRATOR: Music stops
As you board the train, your nose wrinkles at the scent of uncured leather that still clings to the wallet and you smile thinking "Damn that is one strong Fulani cow as you put your Metro Card back in the square hand stitched wallet that Baba had given you years ago, and return it to the deep pockets in your baggy black pants. And at that moment with your hands still on Baji, you spy *him*. He is wearing a pink voluminous robe and leaning on a black umbrella with a wooden handle. You have no doubt that it is he but........

ABOULAYE: Why is my Grandfather dressed in his
ceremonial robes riding the underground in New York
city instead of sitting beneath his fig tree or tending his
beloved cows?

NARRATOR: You put on your train face. You hide
behind a white man's newspaper and cast furtive looks
at your Grandfather who you know is back in Guinea.

(ABOULAYE *prostrates himself at the* NARRATOR's *feet in
the yoga position of "The Child".)*

NARRATOR: You hated going to the bush to visit him
and those cows that he respected like human beings.
You always dreaded the fonio passed around at the
communal meal. Even the family tale of how your
great grandfather, had founded our village, had
brought relatives to raise cattle, become leathersmiths
and thrive on their own labor, did not ease the strange
taste of curdled milk and honey.

"Badaw, do not scorn the cow, whose milk is the
essence of our life, our most powerful medicine, whose
skin protects us. Fulani respects the cow and we
respect one another. Do you understand?"

ABOULAYE: "Yes, Baba."

NARRATOR: "Take this, it is Bagi, who had a red belly
with white flanks. A good milker when she was living
and now she gives us soft leather"

ABOULAYE: That day you put a red and white wallet in
my little hand.

NARRATOR: The train jerks you out of your reverie and
you look for your grandfather's face but instead all you
see is a dapper grey haired man in a pink shirt carrying
a walking stick wondering why you are staring at him.
You get off the train wondering—

ABOULAYE: Is it an angel or a djinn I see on the train? How can that man look so much like Baba and not be a relative?

NARRATOR: In the, in the quarter, in the quarter of the immigrants, languages flow like one dark river rising, Horn of Plenty for those selling by yelling and their shouts are really whispers of a love song in your ears.

ABOULAYE: Check it out checkit out check it out, mamacita papi Yo! Linda, Linda besame. Shoe laces one for fifteen cents two for forty-five grande grande one size fits all sidewalks bleeding money gotta be there to catch the flow. The great God Shango, drying out from bloody seas, sells incense two for dollar brand if you please. Bangladesh and Senegalese, Vietnamese, Mung dark as me, Thailand and Bangkok, Singapore, El Salvador, Guinea, Sierra Leonians, Nigerians, Liberians and Haitians, (those who made it) got rid of tyrant yesterdaddy and here he comes again today, guns and no butter starvation just a bullet away and oppression in all homelands is just about the same, casts a long, long shadow and adds sadness to all songs. Money, money it takes money to send to home.

NARRATOR: But where are the Albanians from Kosovar and other Eurpeans, near and far, who like you seeks succor from Miss Liberty's hand? Not in your neighborhood not in the crossroads of the immigrants and dark natives looking for cheap buys. They are melted in the mainstreams of the land. They are welcomed in Fort Dix by the hand of Hillary who pumps up soft pillows on their individual beds for their ease in spotless sunwashed rooms wired for computers as they eat musaka me patate and I N S begs them (through a translator) to apply within the year for permanent resident status, thank you please. Hurry down the long street to the small space you rent to sell your wares through streets paved with 14

karat gold chains and wiggling electric hula dancers.
Past Japan Express, Camera & Electronics, The Beeper
Zone, Export Specialists, Bedspreads, Curtains, We
Ship Anywhere. Apple green and precious pink taffeta
and tulle waving in the air on wire hangers outside a
store and brass studded trunks spilling into the street
making it difficult for you to navigate on the street of
immigrants paved with gold chains in the crossroads
of Liberty & Opportunity where one size does not fit
all.

(BASSIST: *A long, long interval of music reflecting, the
briskness of trade, the various ethnicities, tempo and tone of
New York's 14th street.)*

NARRATOR: Afternoon prayer-three to four P M.

(Music diminishes, then stops.)

ABOULAYE: Checkitoutcheck itout checkit out check it
out

NARRATOR: *Que bola acere,* my mainman, Whassup?

ABOULAYE: Nada, everything is everything as they say.

NARRATOR: Got to come uptown, Mister. Africa.

ABOULAYE: Downtown is good, rent cheap, business
high? You buy? No problem! Ovah here, checkit out
check it out right this way Mamacita, ay papi Dooney
& Bourke, Coach, Polo Scarves. Wool caps, sunglasses
for winter sunshine
Kungfu tapes, Di Caprio all cheap videos, *regardez ici*
Your Lotto number's coming out if you get ticket here
American Value Center
Nice earrings you try on sistah you like? special price
just for you today

NARRATOR: My Guinean brother, how are you today.
How are the people of Africa?

ABOULAYE: The people of Africa are fine brother man.

Checkit out check out batteries, cassettes socks and ties
And I am fine today also.
T shirts hand dyed, gloves, cigarette lighters
Merci, danke, spasibo, arigato and gracias.
On sale, Manhattan Island, China town, Statue of
Liberty
Rockefeller Center and Radio City, for you my friend
toss in Brooklyn Bridge, A New York Bargain. Five
postcards for one dollar. One dollar bargain.
Everything cheap and looking's free. You like? Take
this shirt, American Cousin.

NARRATOR: For me. Why, Mister Africa?

ABOULAYE: Because my Baba always says kindness is
the greatest wisdom.
Because you look like my old Baba. Beacue I've been
seeing my Grandfather all day, he follows me from
Africa in the faces of you African-black American-
Africans

NARRATOR: Yeah Bro, We part of you, our long lost
people, Maybe even relatives my man. If only we
knew.
Your last prayer of the day.

(BASSIST: *An interval of evening-sunset music that
diminishes before the next speaker.*)

ABOULAYE: This time I am sure. It is Baba riding with
me on the midnight train to the Bronx even though
I am are just as sure he is still back in Guinea. At the
end of the car he sits and stares at me. Between dozes
I stare at him and smile. Now I am not afraid. His face
is a familiar place made strange by the passage of time.
When I get off the train and look around for him I am
not afraid. Maybe grandfather will materialize again
and maybe just stay at my side. After all it's silly to be
afraid of my own flesh and blood. Isn't it?

NARRATOR: You are anxious to get home but you do know not to run or even walk fast for the swarmy night air is swirling with police but it is hard for you are so hungry and all you want to do is hurry home and eat.

ABOULAYE: White rice and a spicy vegetable sauce. Tsibejenne. Mmmmmmmand a dripping sweet mango.

NARRATOR: With your mind already home, you grow hungrier by the minute. As you near your building you look up and of course the woman above you sits as usual perched in her window. What is she looking at, what does she see? *You are thirsty.*

ABOULAYE: Bissop. Tsibejenne. Mmmmmmmmmm.

NARRATOR: In other times, other places you drank cocoanut milk or sugar cane juice but it is a cold drink of bright red bissop that you want right now.

(BASSIST: *A bloodcurdling wailing high note that cannot be mistaken for anything else but a police sirens)*

ABOULAYE & NARRATOR: OOOOOOOOOOOOOOOOOOOOOOOOO!!!! I am standing in the closet size vestibule of my doll house apartment building with my key halfway in the lock when

(Again the blood curdling scream from the Saxophonist [BASSIST?] *accompanied by)*

ABOULAYE & NARRATOR: OOOOOOOOOOOOO!!!

NARRATOR: You are startled at the closeness of the siren scream. Curious, you turn around, warily open the door and look straight into hell.

(BASSIST: *Short stacatto screaming notes evoking "Hell")*

NARRATOR: Eight gunshot eyes and four barking faces. Their decision had already been made. This time it is not Calvary but high on a hill in Northern Manhattan in a place wrested from Indians in the quarter of the

immigrants in a black and tan street of red brick doll
houses.

ABOULAYE: Gunshot faces!

(BASSIST: *Gunshot music*)

ABOULAYE: Barking eyes!
Sptatpataat! Tattatlatlalt! Gotcha!
Gunshotfacesbarking eyesgunshot eyes barking faces!

(BASSIST: *Music evoking the terror of the preceding lines for
several beats*)

NARRATOR: Your eyes grow with terror as large as
history. Sweat and urine pool around your feet like
blood.
At first bullet, Baba, who I know is in Guinea but who
has been hovering around me all day kisses me and
says

(BASSIST: *Three climbing distinct notes, each one higher
than the other, played twice.*)

NARRATOR: "God is great"

ABOULAYE: "Great is God."
First bullet swims in my aorta, bathes in my blood
stream flows to the outposts of my body and is swept
at high bloodtide through my spinal cord. At this point
there is hope. If I live I will be a paraplegic but Baba
grabs my hand saying
"Courage Badaw. The evil djinns have made up their
minds. The speed of their bullets is a hunded meters
per second

NARRATOR: If you could run at that speed you could
cover the length of a football field in about one second.
It will be quic—"

ABOULAYE: Before the old man can finish his words,
inside the miniscule foyer, my gory sky becomes a
crackling hailstorm. Second bullet enters my upper left

side under my arm pit and hurtles downward through
my right kidney, exits out of my back as the next one
enters the left kidney and travels up my right lung at
the same time the third one enters my arm in the front
and leaves in the back almost colliding with this one
now crashing through my collar bone rushing to the
opposite side as if making room for the next bullet
that smashes my chest and rests a millisecond before
exiting out the back of—

NARRATOR: what used to be me and this one
richocheting towards me will enter my side and travel
to the right side passing through my intestines in a
clean straight line unlike the next bullet that leaves
a trail of bone shards and mangled flesh as it travels
a rugged path from my upper thigh to my groin
followed by one that cuts a jagged path in my other
upper thigh but this lazy bullet just rests there and
sleeps unlike this next one that cuts a bloody trail

ABOULAYE & NARRATOR: To the knee bone to the shin
bone to the ankle bone on the left side or this one now
on the right side that comes in below the knee and
takes a short quick trip to my knee bone on my left side
while two more bullets make contact with my left side
again in my left side again, and

ABOULAYE: in my left side again rupturing my spleen,
kidney and any intestines I have left and this last one
puts a hole in my right sole, passing from the bottom of
my feet through my middle toe and through the top of
my right foot turning off my glow-in-the dark sneaker!

NARRATOR: Your breath is shot, bullet riddled. Your
lips like wine. Your stomach pours into the ground
Now you are trains and stars, the shape of change.
Now you are a giant and as you die they love you...

(The two men become one-stand back to back and begin revolving, facing the audience and continue to revolve until they seem to melt into one another as ABOULAYE *speaks:)*

ABOULAYE: One of the four djinns kneels besides me and begs me not to die but Baba has already taken me back to Guinea. Now, I am the siren sound in the gory midnight as I circle between Africa and America, East and West, Earth and Sky, wailing for the green ones who cannot drink water, a clamoring frenzy for the unquenchable thirst for those in sapless lands, a thrumming for parched youths with green mouths and purple lips in a strange land with no succor. Now, I am the plangent song of elders who must return their young to a haunting heritage in a dessicated land. Now, I am kneeling between a ravine and a skyscraper, ululating between the Gambia and the Hudson, rising, falling, floating, pealing, tolling while a woman in the window sits and stares not believing her eyes

*(*BASSIST*: Plays and plays and plays until…)*

(Curtain)

END OF PLAY

UPTOWN!

A TragiComedy

UPTOWN! was first produced by Perishable Theater (Mark Lerman, Artistic Director) in Providence Rhode Island from 12 April-17 May 2003. The cast and creative contributors were:

PSYCHE .... Mark Anthony Brown
OPAL ....Pamela Lambert

Musician ....Rick Massino

Director .... Don Mays
Designer .... Monica Shinn

CHARACTERS & SETTING

OPAL, *an African American Woman*
PSYCHE, *an Afro-American Man*

Bassist is a passenger with a huge bass fiddle

Bus Driver's Voice (Bus Driver and Bus Passengers are huge cardboard images)

Place: A bus headed uptown

PLAYWRIGHT'S NOTES

The BASSIST is silent—his bass is his voice. he has great fun eavesdropping and plays his reaction, seeming to enter the conversation through his music. his reactions and his bass playing should run the gamut between sadness, humor, angry, confusion, fear and love.

(A crawling crowded bus headed uptown in the host city.
BASSIST *is seated on the bus.)*

*(*BASSIST*: Opening Solo of upbeat traveling blues)*

*(The bus is dimly lighted. Bus passengers move in slow
motion on and off the bus. There is something ghostly,
unreal, macabre about them. The Bus Driver could be a huge
papier mache figure with a leering grin. Once in a while
the bus jerks and coughs, throwing passengers together,
entangling their bodies. The bus is already crowded except
for one empty seat, although some folks are already standing.
Suddenly, the bus doors yawn open and in the ritualistic
getting on and off.)*

*(*BASSIST*: Changes music to imitate* PSYCHE*'s scatting,
walking as he enters.)*

*(*PSYCHE *is of indeterminate age. He walks erratically, in the
manner of a wino, Spying the empty seat he makes a beeline
for it. Passengers slowly turn their faces toward him. Once*
PSYCHE *captures the seat, he looks around, stretches his
body, sticking his legs straight out in front of him despite
the crowd and crosses them at the ankles, and folds his hands
across his chest, laying his chin there and closing his eyes.)*

*(*OPAL *enters. She is dressed in New York chic-African-
arts-and-crafts-fashion. She carries a large portfolio. Spying
an empty strap in front of* PSYCHE*, she looks around to see
if she has any other alternative. Seeing none, she settles for
the spot in front of* PSYCHE*. Finally, straddling the large
portfolio between her legs, she extracts a book with one hand,
and hanging onto a strap she proceeds to read in order to
blank out* PSYCHE *in front of her.)*

PSYCHE: Dja wanna sit down?

(Music stops.)

*(*OPAL *ignores* PSYCHE.*)*

PSYCHE: Lady, dja wanna seat?

OPAL: *(Recoiling at his touch)* Ohhhhhhh!

PSYCHE: Look, lady, I was jesh trying to be a gennulman but if you don't want to sit down…fuck it. *(Begins to scat a bebop riff)*

OPAL: Oh no thanks…that's all right.

PSYCHE: Suit yourself…suit yourself. *(Continues scatting. Annoyed that* OPAL *has refused his chivalry, he opens his eyes and delibertly stares at her for a few beats. Suddenly, breaking into a smile, he slowly extracts a bottle form his chest. Ceremoniously opening it, he takes a long slow drink, tilting his head back as far as he can, drinks deeply. Satisfied, he suddenly sits upright.)* Say, Lady, dja wanna drink?

OPAL: Look, I don't want to sit down, I don't want a drink, and I don't want to talk. Now will you please stop? Besides…you're DRUNK!

PSYCHE: Madam…I admit…I did imbibe...I acknowledge that I did partake of the grape. But to accuse me of being inebriated is to slander my character!
(Bus Passengers crack up at both OPAL *and* PSYCHE.*)*

OPAL: I mean, why…why me? All the people on the bus for you to mess with, why do you have to PICK ON ME?

PSYCHE: Lisson, Lady, I thought with all these packages you would be both tired and thirsty…that's all…I didn't meant no harm… Don't you understand? When you are tired you rest.
(Music: high notes to low notes)

PSYCHE: When you are thirsty you drink

I jes ask you to sit an have a lil ole drink with me.......
that's all.
(Upbeat intoxicated blues)
(OPAL retreats to her book.)

PSYCHE: What chu reading, lady?
(OPAL continues to ignore PSYCHE.)

PSYCHE: Don't ig me, woman.
(Music stops playing)

PSYCHE: I don't unnerstan how you could hang all over
me...knocking up against me and me sitting in front of
you, eye level to your crotch
(Music: lurid short note)

PSYCHE: and you still pretend that I'm not real. I SAY,
WHAT ARE YOU READING?

OPAL *(Coldly)* You're sure. You're quite sure you want
to have a conversation with me?

PSYCHE: What better way for an old drunk riding
uptown on a bus to pass his years than to have a
conversation with a young lady with clear eyes?

OPAL: You are sure. You are quite sure its just not your
liquor talking?

PSYCHE: Madam...I do feel its my duty to tell you...my
liquor is me. When I speak...the grapes speaks... We
are inseparable...
*(At this point the bus jerks...throwing OPAL into PSYCHE's
lap. He holds his arms out to her as she scrambles, trying to
recover her composure.)*

OPAL: Elimination of the Sexes: Toward an
Androgynous Society
(Music: short, low, menacing notes)

OPAL: The title of the book...I mean...

PSYCHE: The title's enough to make me lose my high...

OPAL: This book is really great. I think in order to be a total person—

PSYCHE: Ahhhh, I get you, baby. You a big freak, huh. That's okay, some of my best friends...

OPAL: I'm not talking about lust. Once we eliminate false divisions such as male and female then we can start to relate to each other as people!

PSYCHE: Uh huh.

OPAL: Look, why do you think I refused your offer of a seat? Because you are a drunken bum? No. Of course not. I'm not like that. It's because you only offered me a seat because I'm a woman!

PSYCHE: Look...I only thought...

OPAL: All of these men standing and you didn't offer them a seat. Oh, I know what you automatically thought through your drunken stupor. "Poor Lady". You felt sorry for me because I am a woman when the truth is you need the seat more than I do!

PSYCHE: If you want the truth lady, I didn't want you blocking my view with all your packages. I didn't want that thing with the sharp edges slowly boring a hole in my knee like it's doing at this moment!

OPAL: *(Moving the portfolio quickly away from* PSYCHE*'s knee)* Oh. I am sorry.

PSYCHE: What's in that thing, anyhow?

OPAL: My sketches.

*(*PSYCHE *just looks at* OPAL, *saying nothing.)*

OPAL: Aren't you going to ask me about them? You were the one with all the questions a few seconds ago.

PSYCHE: Yeah. That was before I felt like an endangered species.

(Music: Menacing low to high)

OPAL: I'm a designer…I design intersex clothes for the human body. Here, let me show you what I mean… *(Manages to open the portfolio)* Here's my biggest item… pants on one leg and skirt on the other… Isn't that lovely… And here's my open-toed high heel shoes for both men and women…

PSYCHE: Look. Lady, you win…I withdraw my offer of a conversation.

(Music: 12 Bar Blues)

PSYCHE: So WILL YOU PLEASE STOP? I withdraw my offer of a seat. STAND. You can stand there until you grow roots…stand there till the hairs on your pussy turn gray… You can…

OPAL: YOU DRUNKEN BUM! YOU ARE CRUDE! CRUEL! VULGAR!

PSYCHE: SAVAGE! SADISTIC! SALACIOUS! The nation's nightmare! Everything you invented. The demon you dream of. The Black male heard in modern myth! Look, it's only me, Psyche….what's your name? *(OPAL does not answer.)*

PSYCHE: Lilith? Eve? Hagar? Jezebel? Delilah? *(Music: Punctuates each name…low bend at last name.)*

OPAL: They were all wicked whores and witches!

PSYCHE: Kali? Fatima? Isis?

OPAL: They were all goddesses.

PSYCHE: Which one are you? Let me see. What do you ladies call yourselves these days? Kadeejha? Sayeeda? Naima? I mean, what can I do with a name? Can I hock it? Please, baby. Tell me your name. Ohhhh ha! I get it… You're afraid I'll find you in the telephone book and make "Hello, baby, you wanna fuck?" phone calls to you…

OPAL: OPAL! MY NAME IS OPAL!

PSYCHE: *(Tipping his hat and bowing slightly)* Pleased to meet you, Miss Opal... You didn't ask me what my name is but I'm Psyche. Now that we're on a first name basis, Miss Opal...tell me...where do you live? That's right. Speak right up.

OPAL: UPTOWN. I live uptown.

PSYCHE: Where uptown? Oh, come on...I'm not in any frame of mind to rob you tonight. What street?

OPAL: Uptown.

PSYCHE: Lenox? Seventh? Eight?

OPAL: Of course not! Convent. Convent Avenue.

PSYCHE: Of course. Convent Avenue. Ritzy, ain't we?

OPAL: Relative. Everything is relative. I suppose from your vantage point it would look good to you.

PSYCHE: I'll ignore that. Now that we're getting along just fine, I'll pretend I didn't hear that cutting remark. Apartment?

OPAL: Brownstone.

PSYCHE: Own? Rent?

OPAL: Own.

PSYCHE: What street?

OPAL: One Hundred Forty-Fifth Street.

PSYCHE: I bet it's that house on the corner.

OPAL: *(Challengingly)* Which corner? Which house?

PSYCHE: Northeast corner. The house with the brown shutters, I bet.

OPAL: How...

PSYCHE: And the white awnings?

OPAL: ...did...

PSYCHE: With the window box of red geraniums?

OPAL: ...you...

PSYCHE: With the iron door with filigree.

OPAL: How did you know? You described my house
exactly. Who are you, anyhow?

PSYCHE: Taking out his bottle and putting it to his
head, wipes his lips with the back of his hand
(Music: Tipsy music)

PSYCHE: Look, lady...I'm just a drunken tramp riding
the bus uptown. I do a lot of walking uptown...see a
lot of houses. Some I remember. Some I don't. No big
deal... Besides...you talk too much.
(Music: Three shot high "laugh" notes)

OPAL: What? Mister...Psyche...you are crazy!

PSYCHE: Is that a medical or lay opinion? NO matter. I
reject it.

OPAL: Look, Mister...whatever you call yourself. Who
are you? What do you do?

PSYCHE: Anything...I'll do anything. But we're not
discussing me....at least not yet. Let's stick to you since
you're the one that's hanging over me. Know what I
could do to you? It's so crowded in here all I have to do
is stick out my tongue...
(Music: Painting, breathing lurid)

OPAL: No!

PSYCHE: No? then tell me, Opal. Tell me. Who do you
live with in that big house on the northeast corner with
the white awnings. NO. Don't tell me. I'll tell you.
Your husband. He's a dull man with a high salary who
you married for his potential.
(OPAL is silent.)
(Music: Dull low, wah wah)

PSYCHE: No? Then you have children.

(Music: Fast high children sounds)

PSYCHE: No. If you do it's just one.

(Music: One note)

PSYCHE: Isn't it. A boy.

(Music: One lower note)

PSYCHE: I bet. It happened before you were married. But you didn't let it prevent you from being a colored success.

(OPAL *remains silent.*)

PSYCHE: Your parents? No...it couldn't be... You left them in some tedious town in their prefabricated mortgage. You came to New York so that you could be loudly anonymous.

OPAL: For your information, Mister Psyche...I live alone.

PSYCHE: But you have several cats.

(Music: Soft meow sound)

OPAL: One...just one.

(Music stops.)

OPAL: Dog, that is. Great Dame.

(Music: Low growl)

PSYCHE: I bet he's male.

OPAL: Yes. His name is Niger.

PSYCHE: And you have papers on him.

OPAL: Ad I have papers on him.

PSYCHE: And you have a special butcher where you buy forty pounds weekly of the choicest music for doggie. You take your tamed wolf to shows where he struts

(Music: Strutting notes)

PSYCHE: and wins ribbons for you. He licks your face at night in place of everything else.

OPAL: How did you know about Niger's ribbons? ...I thought you looked familiar. You must have been at the last dog show.

PSYCHE: I was...I was first prize. Arf, arf.
(Music: Imitates PSYCHE *barking and howling)*

OPAL: Why are you rambling on like this?

PSYCHE: Tell me more about you and Niger.

OPAL: Oh, I forgot to tell you about Ronnie, and Herbert, Yusef, David, and Bob. They live with me also.

PSYCHE: Aha!

OPAL: Sure...they're my plants... Poor Ronnie...he's the fern and he's always thirsty and has to be watered constantly but the Swedish ivy, philodendrons, ficus, and red geraniums in the window box are doing fine, thank you.

PSYCHE: You, the dog, and the plants.

OPAL: You know, before I got the hang of it I used to just look at a plant and he would die. Now, I've finally got the knack of growing them. But before I cultivated my green thumb I would call myself "the Plantkiller."

PSYCHE: *(Looks at* OPAL *for a few beats)* I'm getting off right now.
(Music: Yelling and screaming notes, reflecting PSYCHE's *terror)*

PSYCHE: *(Yelling)* Goddammit, bus driver. Stop this bus right now. I WANT TO GET OFF!

OPAL: *(Shoving him back in his seat)* No! You can't leave now. I haven't finished telling you about myself.

PSYCHE: Opal…I know all about you. Every nook and cranny of you.

OPAL: Don't' be too sure. I'm translucent but not transparent. Opal throws off lights in different colors and shapes. How can you be so sure of what you're seeing when you look at me?

PSYCHE: *(Takes out his bottle and holds it out in front of him, looking through it as if it's a crystal ball.)* Oh…I can see right through you. We know each other. I just didn't want to live through it again tonight but… *(Puts cap on the bottle decisively after taking a swig and continues)* …yes, Opal. I know you. For instance…let me tell you what you'll do when you get off this bus. As soon as you step off this bus you will put a curse on it, hoping that it smashes to smithereens before the next stop, and tell yourself that you really must take a cap next time in order to avoid drunks like me. You will walk along the streets, hugging the curb, afraid, looking at the unlighted eyes of men that grow form sidewalks like bent trees. Secretly laughing when they sing their broken songs or dance. You hurry away from them, stepping on broken tears while avoiding the dog shit. You will hide your flesh form some passing admirer, denying him the magic of lust. But your juice overflows and hiding inside your face, you lurk behind your eyes, measuring the plants of each man passing by, secretly snapping off his penis and spitting it into your perfumed hankie, coughing daintily, pretending you have a cold! Making your way to your house, you curse the air, wishing you were somewhere else, but some radical teacher in New England college nestled in the peaceful Berkshire mountains told you the ghetto was your battlefield so here you remain, hunting for a Black puritan. Destroying every man that is not the freak of your imagination. You will finally reach your house and put the key in your door, looking over your

shoulder to make sure that one of those men whose joint you stole is not following you.
(Music: Trill up slowly anticipatory notes)

OPAL: Oh, ha, ha, ha, ha, ha, ha!
(Music: Echo laughing)

OPAL: You're a funny man…you know. A very funny man. I DON'T WANT TO HEAR ANY MORE!

PSYCHE: You're right, Miss Opal. Excuse me…it must be my liquor talking. You got to forgive an old drunk… riding the bus uptown.

OPAL: You tramp. You bum. You wino. How dare you talk to met his way? Don't' you know I can have you arrested?

PSYCHE: Sure you can. You can do that… You're the woman to do it.

OPAL: *(Looking around impatiently)* Oh God! Oh God! Oh God! This bus is so slow!

PSYCHE: Easy, baby, easy. Can't wait to get off, huh? Can't wait to send this bus smashing straight to hell, huh? *(Laughing)* I can't blame you… If I had to stand as long as you have, talking to someone like me with no room to get away from him…I'd feel the same way. Don't' you want to hear what happens next?

OPAL: When?

PSYCHE: When you put your keys inside the door. Don't you want to hear what you'll do once you get inside your house?

OPAL: That's enough, Mister. I've listened to you for long enough. Who are you?
(Music: Quiet ballad played softly until PSYCHE closes his eyes, doesn't answer.)

OPAL: *(Leaning close to him, whispering)* You can't fool me anymore. Every shit eye ain't asleep. Every red eye

ain't drunk. So you know who I am…well, you are
right. There is something in me so empty, so longing,
so full of pain and rage that I hesitate to speak, for
fear of being discovered. But you recognized me and I
know who you are too.

PSYCHE: But we're not talking about me…at least not
yet…so you tell me. What *will* you do?

OPAL: I will put the key in my iron door with the
filigree on it and shut it against the day. I will pace the
rooms of my empty house and laugh at how you were
on this bus, undressing me with your smile. I will run
my hands over my body and scratch my left nipple,
(Music stops.)

OPAL: thinking of the men I made heavy with
lust as I passed them by. I'll conjure up images of
several possible lovers. I'll feed Niger and watch his
flanks shiver in appreciation and wonder why all
relationships can't be as simple. I'll water my plants
and pay special attention to Ronnie. Poor Ronnie. I lied
about him. I told you that he was a fern but he's not.
He's a penis that I cut off and planted in my window
box. He's always thirsty, never satisfied, but when I
feed him he curls up like a prayer plant and takes back
every loving thing he's said to me. Sometimes he flies
around the room, following me to bed. When I put him
back in his pot, he cries. And finally, I sing….
(Music: A blue tune to accompany OPAL.)

OPAL: I gave my love a poem
I gave my love a baby
He said thank you for the poem
Thank you for the baby chile
I love you sweetcakes
But I'm gonna leave for a while
And so Mister Psyche, or whatever your name is….
because of the men who beat their heads against the

sidewalk and mumble in unknown tongues whenever
I come near them, because of the lover who passes me
by with blood in his eyes, an emptiness gorws, silent
and cruel…but what about you? You haven't told me
where you live but I know… You're going to the last
stop, to the end of the line…and then you'll start all
over again… There's no address, no number for you…
you're free. You sit there in your freedom, having
nothing, wanting anything I have, wanting to be me—

PSYCHE: *(Jumps up from the seat and pulls* OPAL *down,
throwing her into the seat)* SIT DOWN…NOW YOU SIT
YOUR ASS DOWN!

OPAL: I know who you are, I know who you are, I
know who you are, I know who you are!

(Music echoes "I know who you are")

PSYCIIE: *(Removes his disguise, reveals a handsome, healthy,
sober man)* SHUT UP AND LET ME SPEAK. I don't
own one house with one dog, several plants, and a
potted penis. I have no home. Not New York, America,
or Africa. What I do have is several different places
to stay, depending on what mood folks are in. And
in one of those places, I don't remember which one
at the moment, is my briefcase and in that briefcase
are…let's see…numerous bits of paper with names
and numbers that have lost their meaning…some
eight by ten glossies showing several of my faces. See,
I'm an actor in this world, constantly adjusting to my
surroundings. Some "Get out and take your things"
letters from women who have begun to catch on that I
am only passing through… OH, don't get me wrong…
there's nothing wrong with you ladies except that you
want me to act out yoru soap opera fantasies and I
can't say who I am unless you agree that I'm real but
you don't want me to be real…. And in that briefcase
in one of those places, I can't remember where, are
my dreams…. You call me bum with no ambition?

Baby…I have dreamed empires into existence! You're right; having nothing myself, I want what you got, I want the world, I want the universe. Some nerve for a nigger, huh? You got on this bus and all you could see was a tramp. But I wear disguises so that I can watch the world watch me. My disguises protect my tender insides from the vulgar tongue, from the hard eyes of dream killers, from women like you. *(Goes into his drunken act)* Dja wanna drink, lady, keep it moving, keep it moving. Hello, Dolly, this is Satchmo, darling… *(Music imitates* PSYCHE.)

PSYCHE: …the names you call me are not mine… The face you see is only a mask. Look at me… Look at me… Are you willing? Do you dare? This is a recording… Leave your answer and get off the bus! *(Sits down wearily in an empty seat next to* OPAL)

OPAL: *(Softly)* I'm thirsty
(Music: Long interval of quiet, romantic, sensual underneath the following:)

PSYCHE: Have a drink…of water *(He hands* OPAL *his bottle.)*

OPAL: *(Takes a long slow drink)* Ahhh. That is good. There is seeing and being seen. Which one are you frightened of?

PSYCHE: I want to be seen… Can you see me?

OPAL: Will you come home with me?

PSYCHE: Sure, why not… I came when called, go when chased, am grateful when fed.

OPAL: You don't love… You don't hate… There's no such thing as feeling?

PSYCHE: I could hold your hand. And smile at you. I know what. We'll pretend we just met.

OPAL: I'll find myself in your face. In your body.

PSYCHE: I'll see you in the sunlight.

OPAL: We'll smile at each other through the day and night. We'll be a mirror facing each other.

OPAL & PSYCHE: Let's dance.

(Music continues the same tune)

(OPAL and PSYCHE stand up and face each other. They do a weird sensuous dance stalking each other but do not touch.)

PSYCHE: What were you afraid of?

OPAL: You...me...them... *(Indicating Bus Passengers)* What will you do if they find out we love each other?

PSYCHE: NO. WE CAN'T. STOP IT.

(Music stops.)

PSYCHE: IT'S USELESS. I don't want you to see me. I know how they see me. But you, you must not see me that way. Don't' you understand? That's why I keep running away. I'm running away from you very fast. Because I know what you see.

(Music: Low ballad church chord underneath the following:)

PSYCHE: You see a body without power
A mind without dreams
A man without his name
We're dead to each other before love is born
We're dead to each other before love is born
If they take away your body, you can't work
If they take away your mind, you can't dream
I can work
I can dream
I can't love you!

OPAL: I'm dead to the world
But I've never been born
We're dead to each other
Before love is born
Then world sees a place
To hide its dark desire

You see
Eyes without light
Lips without a song
A woman
Without beauty
I am thirsty
I must drink
I am hungry
I must eat
I will eat
I will drink
(Music stops.)

OPAL: I won't love you!

(OPAL and PSYCHE retreat into their separate worlds trying to ignore each other.)
(Music: The opening blues solo for a long time and then silence)

PSYCHE: D'ja wanna drink?
(Curtain)

END OF PLAY

www.ingramcontent.com/pod-product-compliance
Lightning Source LLC
Chambersburg PA
CBHW070033110426
42741CB00035B/2754